"We all know about the Christmas tree, the turkey, the tinsel, the presents and even the carol services. But what's it all really about? Let the book in your hand lead you past all the trappings to the astonishing truth of the authentic Christmas story, so helpfully explained here. You'll never regret taking the time to investigate."

TERRY VIRGO, Founder of NewFrontiers; Author of *Life Tastes Better*

"While engaging with some of our favorite holiday traditions, Andrew invites us to consider the plausibility of the story of the first Christmas. He explores the historical narratives of Jesus as Light, Savior and King while sharing family stories that make you feel like a guest in the Wilson home for the holidays. What a fun and helpful read!"

VANESSA K. HAWKINS, Director of Community Life, Redeemer Lincoln Square, Manhattan

"A wonderful book that connects so many of our contemporary Christmas experiences to the story of the very first Christmas. A must-read for anyone seeking to understand the deeper meaning of Christmas or for those of us who have become a little too familiar with the story and need to rediscover the wonder of it all."

GAVIN CALVER, CEO of the Evangelical Alliance

GW00648271

"Christmas is a highlight of my year. It's always sad when it's over. But what if Christmas also has the power to transform our normal lives into something super-normal? This book unlocks this power. Check it out and see how the miracle of Christmas doesn't end with the birth of Jesus but can continue to work its joy in our lives today."

SAM CHAN, Head Trainer, EvQ and City Bible Forum, Australia

"This has me feeling Christmassy—in every sense. A gem of a book. If you want to know some festive joy, read this!"

GLEN SCRIVENER, Author of *The Air We Breathe*; Host of the SpeakLife podcast

It's

Beginning

to Look a Lot

Like Christmas

ANDREW
WILSON

It's Beginning to Look a Lot Like Christmas
© Andrew Wilson, 2024.

Published by
The Good Book Company

thegoodbook.com | thegoodbook.co.uk
thegoodbook.com.au | thegoodbook.co.nz | thegoodbook.co.in

Published in association with the literary agency of Wolgemuth & Wilson.

Cover design by Drew McCall

ISBN: 9781802541113 | Printed in India

Contents

Introduction: What Makes Christmas *Christmas*?

Most of us experience a moment when it starts to feel like Christmas. It may be a fixed point that we anticipate eagerly, because without it the Christmas season cannot begin: like the end of Thanksgiving or the start of December or our first sight of the Coca-Cola "holidays are coming" advert. Or it could be a moment which catches us by surprise. Last week I went to Winter Wonderland in London's Hyde Park for the first time, and as I stood in my hat and scarf surrounded by fairy lights and the aroma of mulled wine, it was as if autumn had become Christmas in an instant.

It's hard to describe how those defining moments actually work. In terms of time, no particular day moves Christmas closer than any other. For commercial reasons, big companies spend lots of money trying to make us feel Christmassy as early as possible: carols in the shopping malls in November, festive drinks for sale in October, gift suggestions and boxes of mince pies in September. But although these marketing departments do their best, their efforts don't resonate. Certain things have to happen before we feel that it's really beginning to look a lot like Christmas.

One of the first, where I come from, is the putting up of lights. I live on a small, windswept island in the North Atlantic, just south of the Arctic Circle, and it gets really dark at this time of year; at the start of December, sunrise is at 7:44am and sunset at 3:54pm. But the Christmas lights make it all worth it. The bulbs hanging in crescent-shaped arcs across the streets and the twinkling displays in coffee shops all create an ambience of anticipation. Personally, I don't think it can feel like Christmas until the lights go up all around the place.

Another moment for me is putting up the family Christmas tree. Some years, we have taken a trip to a pub in the middle of nowhere that sells trees as a side hustle and have chosen the largest one that will fit in our car. Other years, we have bought and built a fake tree—borderline illegal to some but undoubtedly quicker, cheaper and tidier. But whether the tree is real or fake, putting it up in the living room starts the season in ways that few other things do. It is soon followed by wreaths, sprigs of holly, and other plants whose names I don't know and am afraid to ask about.

As the great day gets closer, the anticipation intensifies. Somewhere in the day or two beforehand, I find I stop thinking that Christmas is coming and start thinking that Christmas is here. I have my last day at work. Our extended family gathers together for a meal. The present wrapping is finished. Stockings are hung above the fireplace. Christmas movies and TV shows flood the airwaves. By Christmas Eve, four weeks after our children started planning it and four months after the local supermarket started planning it, it is finally and fully looking a lot like Christmas.

Of course, it may be different things for you that make Christmas feel like Christmas. But I bet it's something. I imagine you can list right now what are the joys that make the season feel special for you.

This book aims to persuade you of one thing: that all these Christmas joys only make sense—and in fact *life* only begins to make sense—if we understand the meaning of the first Christmas. It is only in the Bethlehem manger, surrounded by shepherds and wise men and farm animals, that we find the reason for the trees, traditions, tinsel and turkey. But more importantly, it is only in the Bethlehem manger that we find the reason for the deeper things that make life meaningful for the rest of the time. It is only there that we find real hope that the world will one day be filled with peace and justice, love that does not depend on our ability or performance, and joy that can withstand the ups and downs of life.

That idea shapes what follows. In each chapter, I'll introduce you to one of the aspects of this season that makes me feel like it's really Christmas. And we'll use each of those things as a lens through which to look back to the first Christmas and consider the world-changing difference it has made.

And Is It True?

One question that sooner or later overshadows any discussion of the first Christmas, and its talk of God becoming human in the person of Jesus Christ, is whether or not it is true. Did it really happen? Some people look at the miraculous details of the Christmas story—signs in the stars, predictive dreams, supernatural beings, a miraculous conception—and conclude that it cannot possibly be true, however heartwarming or inspiring it is. That may be your perspective. And if it didn't happen, then no amount of wrapping can disguise the fact that the Christian message is empty. But if it did—if the Creator of the world has become human in order to rescue the world from sin and death—then nothing on earth can compare with it, and no amount of tinsel, trees or turkey could be celebration enough.

In the end, you have to decide for yourself. But believing in the truth of this story is not as big a leap as you might think. It is not only ancient people who used the stars to guide them in their life choices, who were sure there was something beyond what we can see and measure, who changed their lives according to particularly striking dreams or who wondered about the meaning of events that could have been coincidences but didn't feel like that.

In fact, I am willing to bet that you yourself believe in all sorts of supernatural entities—things which are "above nature". If you believe in human rights, dignity, equality or justice, then you are a believer in things that can't be seen or proved in a laboratory or test-tube.

And you probably believe in a kind of miraculous conception too, even if we don't call it that. Our generation's current understanding of the cosmos is that the universe suddenly and instantaneously burst into existence around 13.7 billion years ago—a theory that we know as the "Big Bang". There was moment when something came from nothing. There was a moment when life appeared where previously there hadn't been life.

If you are tempted to dismiss the Christmas story for being fanciful, it is worth remembering how many extraordinary things you believe already.

And then consider one more thing: the only way we can be sure there are no miracles is if we can be sure there is no God. If there is an all-powerful Creator of the world, then it makes no sense to declare that he couldn't speak to people in dreams, or light up the sky with angel choirs, or even become flesh and be born of a virgin. If we can be certain there is no God, then we can be certain these things never happened. If we can't, that does not mean these things are all true. But it means they might be. If God is possible, miracles are possible. So it is worth approaching the story with an open mind.

Anything but Ordinary

None of this is to say that the Christmas story is ordinary. It absolutely is not. There is no event more extraordinary than this: that the Creator of this world became part of it, born of a woman whom he designed and breathing air that he made. I would go further, actually: nothing more extraordinary has ever been claimed to have happened. There is some weird stuff on the internet but nothing that compares with the idea that the God who created the Eagle Nebula became a helpless infant.

So it's time to consider that idea by thinking about the ways we get ready for Christmas. And we're going to start with the thing that gets my Christmas started, and indeed gets the whole Bible started. Let there be lights.

1

Putting Up the Lights

Few things can generate excitement in the Wilson household like putting up the Christmas lights. And few things can generate the same levels of bafflement, frustration, technical confusion and abject fury.

In theory it should be an idyllic experience. Sometimes it is. Mince pies are baking; wine is mulling; Diana Krall's Christmas album is playing. The children are excited. The evening is clear. All it takes is a brief trip into the loft to retrieve the box of fairy lights and hang them on the tree, and our Instagrammable Christmas experience will be complete.

The problems start when the box is opened. Somehow the lights, which were carefully stowed last year so as to make removing them easier this year, have been shuffled, shaken, intertwined, and so thoroughly entangled by the loft pixies that they resemble nothing less than a plate of fir-green spaghetti. Disentangling them takes an age, which is long enough for one child to begin pilfering the mince pies and another to remember how much they hate Diana Krall. Hanging them over the tree is always more complicated than I think it is going to be, mainly because the kids have started putting their favourite baubles on it already and because apparently it is vital that the baubles are backlit rather than obscured by the cables. Not only that but the lights come with four hundred and seven different settings—slow fade, rapid twinkle, annoying flicker, epileptic-seizure generator, and so forth—so it takes another age to work out how to turn them on, by which time the mulled wine resembles beetroot soup with a garnish of cinnamon sticks.

Still—at least the lights are on.

Then the Light Came

And we do like light. Most of us by instinct don't particularly like the dark. It makes children feel scared and adults feel sad, especially when it goes on for months. We long for spring in part because brightness makes us feel bright and gloom makes us gloomy. We turn on the lights when we go into a room because we want to know where everything is. We love to see houses festooned with Christmas lights; give me a garish and tastelessly lit-up house over a dark one any day. We are drawn to the light.

All cultures are. The major world religions all have a festival or story that centres on light in some way. Hanukkah is the Jewish festival of light. Hindus celebrate Diwali, which means "row of lights". Buddhists see the aim of life as achieving "enlightenment", by which they mean a moment of discovery in which you stop the endless cycle of reincarnation and reach Nirvana. Islam has the concept of spiritual and intellectual illumination, which is reflected in the way Muslims illuminate manuscripts of the Qur'an. Christians also focus on light, as we will see. Darkness and light are universal human experiences, so the idea that the light has come into the darkness—or that we have turned the lights on in order to banish the darkness—is a very common narrative around the world.

You can see it in ideological and political projects too, from East to West. You may have heard of the Ming dynasty of China, for example, famous for their vases and a pretty impressive wall. "Ming" simply means "brightness"; it was a name that suggested the darkness had been banished and a new regime of light established.

The 21st-century West's version is very similar. Here is how we think about ourselves: the whole world was mired in gloom, ignorance and superstition for centuries (the "Dark Ages"). But then modern Europe experienced a rebirth (the "Renaissance"), and soon people started to think for themselves, ask critical questions, use science, build complex machines, and make everyone richer and healthier (the "Enlightenment"). Things were dark. Then the light came. And everything got better.

Where's Your Light?

We think this way more personally too—about the things that happen in our own lives. You have almost certainly said or heard someone else say at some point, "It's been a dark time". You have almost certainly said or heard someone else say at some point, "Don't worry;there's a light at the end of the tunnel". We talk like this all the time. Darkness is sad, but one day it will be light. In the meantime we need to hold on, hunker down, and hope.

The question, whatever culture and/or religion you feel connected to, is: What's your light? When the world around you, on the global level or the more personal one, is difficult and frustrating and challenging and depressing, what do you look to in order to be able to say, "It's going to be okay"? Where does your mind go to in order to be able to think to yourself, "Yes, this is hard, but I can look to this light to know that this situation will get better. This is where I'll look to find hope." Everyone who is not utterly hopeless has a light. What's yours?

The answer to that question almost certainly depends on what you think the "darkness" is. Unless you have a perfect life (in which case, I'm not sure you're living in the same world as the rest of us), where you look for light will be directed by what you think the root of the problems in your own life or in this world are.

For the Ming in China, the darkness was the instability caused by constant invasion by foreigners. So (and I'm simplifying here!) they built a huge wall and said, "We've solved the problem. The darkness has gone. The brightness has come. Our rule over you will provide all the light you need."

In Buddhism, the darkness is illusion about what is real and what is not, so the light is a moment of realisation about reality.

In the Western story—what you could call secular liberalism—the darkness is ignorance, and so the light is knowledge. That's why, if you grew up in a Western context, you probably think that education will solve most of the problems we face.

Here's why I don't sign up to those views of darkness and light: they all lowball the problem. Ultimately, the darkness in the world is not just about ignorance, or political instability, or a lack of education. It's about death. (Happy Christmas!) The world is dark because people die, spiritually and physically, not just because they don't know enough or because they have been invaded too often. Even in the most educated and least invaded societies in world history, like the 21st-century US or Australia or UK, the darkness of death is still here.

The Bible says that death operates on two levels. The first is the one we tend to think about: namely physical death. But there is also a deeper, spiritual level of death, in which we are separated from God. Put the two together and you have the reason for why we struggle— even in an age when there is more peace and prosperity than ever before—to find fulfilment and security. We know that life is not quite as it should be.

That's pretty dark. But it explains why building a wall or having a spiritual experience or gaining more education and knowledge doesn't provide sufficient light to pierce the darkness. We build our walls; we talk about our religions; we find out more and more; we put our Christmas lights up, enjoy them, take them down again and put them away ready for the next year. Yet true light, inner peace, deep joy, steadfast love... these things remain elusive to us, personally and globally. The darkness of death is still here.

So what do we need? We need a light that can banish death and restore us to life, spiritually and physically.

The Light from Beyond

People often think that the Christmas story is schmaltzy and sentimental. Many of us see it as a story for children. In the West, we put Jesus in the crib alongside Santa in his sleigh: a nice childish tale which gives us a good reason to take a holiday, eat, drink, and have a rest. Angels, mangers, carols and trees are nice and sparkly and comforting—twinkly reassurances at the most wonderful time of the year.

In fact, though, the Christmas story is a brutally honest account of how dark the world really is. It takes place in a land occupied by a foreign army, among a people burdened by taxes and dreaming of freedom. Its central characters are mostly on the margins of society, far from the palaces and universities where life is warm and exciting and light. It ends—although we usually leave this part out of our modern versions—with a power struggle that leaves dozens of young children murdered and Jesus' family fleeing as refugees. The Christmas story in the Bible is very real about the darkness in this world.

Yet the Bible is also very confident in its claim that at Christmas, Light came into the world. It didn't come from within this world, as though we can fix our own problems. It didn't come by looking within us or around us but by looking beyond us, to a source of light from outside this world. At the first Christmas, Light stepped into the darkness in person: a Light that "shines in the darkness, and the darkness has not overcome it". At the first Christmas, "the true light, which gives light to everyone, was coming into the world" (from the Bible— the Gospel of John, chapter 1, verses 5 and 9).

The Light which shone at that first Christmas has been shining defiantly in the face of darkness for two thousand years and is still shining today. This

Light does not look like a giant wall along the border of China or a Western university full of clever people doing experiments or a man sitting cross-legged with a lotus flower in front of him. It looks like a dark-haired, dark-eyed Jewish baby in the arms of his unmarried teenage mother. This is Jesus Christ—the one Christians call the Light of the world.

So why is this baby, among the millions of others born that year and the billions of others born through history, the Light? What does this Light do? And can it—can he—really make a difference in your life today? That's what this book is about.

2

Time with Family

Christmas is a time to honour your ancestors. Generally we don't think about it that way, but most of us do it all the same; we get the children, the parents and the grandparents (and possibly even the great-grandparents) together in one place, no matter how convoluted or squished it makes our Christmas dinner. These days, for my family that means 22 of us converging on a cul-de-sac in Sussex, England. When I was a child, it meant a six-hour drive to the far end of Cornwall and the south-western tip of Britain, followed by a six-hour conversation between my parents and my grandparents about whether we could have got there quicker if we had taken a different route.

Most families in history have had far more contact between ancestors and descendants than people do in the West today. I grew up seeing my grandparents just once or twice a year. But Christmas is one moment when it is quite normal to pull together all the generations. Retired businessmen pull crackers, wear paper crowns and blow party whistles at toddlers; retired nursery teachers get nerf guns out and fire them at teenagers. For a couple of days, we remember that despite our enormous differences in age and experience, we are all related in one giant family tree and all part—for better and worse—of one shared, ongoing story that stretches back into history and (we hope) will stretch forwards into the future.

Agatha Christie and Me

Most families contain some people we're proud to be associated with and some people who, if we're honest, we find it a bit awkward to be connected to.

In my family, one great source of ancestral pride is my great-grandfather. Wilfred Pirie was a sub-lieutenant in the Royal Navy, who won the Distinguished Service Order for leading a small fleet of British submarines across the Atlantic in 1915. (That was pretty brave, by the way. Crewing a submarine in 1915 was about as safe as sailing a rubber duck.) Not only that; he proposed to Agatha Christie. The best-selling fiction writer in history described him as "an immense friend at once, one of the people in my life I have been fondest of ... we were unofficially engaged." But before long, she had second thoughts and broke off the relationship.

"With him there was no excitement ... the prospect of marrying Wilfred induced in me a depressing feeling of boredom," she explained in her autobiography (a bit harshly, I think). "I still feel I was a monster of ingratitude not to have married him."

Wilfred Pirie is a name I know because he was my great-grandfather, and because he was a war hero who connects me (if only through rejection) to a famous author. But at the same time, as I was writing this, I realised I didn't know the first names of all my other great-grandparents. Give yourself a quick test: do you? Could you name all eight of your great-grandparents off the top of your head?

My suspicion is that we only remember particular members of our family tree if they did something of particular significance. Perhaps they did something particularly noble, or won a medal, or moved to the country in which we now live, or gave us our first or middle name. Maybe they narrowly missed out on marriage to a multimillion-selling author. If you were to have a king or queen in your line, you'd probably know that and talk about it. On the other hand, you'd be unlikely to talk about the woman in your line who had a one-night stand with a stranger and ended up pregnant, or the guy who had sex with her and was never heard of again.

We tend to weight our family stories towards the famous or the impressive. We often focus on the good news stories, whether they are long-deceased names in a family tree or people who are very much alive today. And we avoid mention of the parts of the family who are harder work or come with complexities.

When it comes to the family tree of the baby who was born at the first Christmas, though, the Bible does the opposite.

Family Pride and Family Shame

In first-century Jewish culture, family trees really mattered. (People would have known the names of their great-grandparents.) If you or I were writing up the life story of Jesus, we would likely not have begun with a family tree. But for Matthew, a Jewish guy who knew Jesus well when Jesus was an adult and who gave his name to the book in the Bible that we now call "Matthew's Gospel", it made perfect sense within his culture to start his account with a genealogy that stretches back almost 50 generations.

Another thing that really mattered in first-century Jewish culture was shame. So if you wanted to present yourself or your friend in a positive way, you would weight the family story towards those ancestors whose reputations were good, and you would keep quiet about any scandal or mess. And, since this was a patriarchal society, what mattered most was the men you were descended from.

So what is strange about the first sixteen verses of Matthew's Gospel is not that he begins with a family tree but that he breaks the rules. As he traces Jesus' line, Matthew deliberately and unnecessarily includes five women, all of whom bore the taint of scandal.

You may or may not recognise their names, but if you'd been reading in the first century, you definitely would have:

- Tamar: a woman who pretended to be a prostitute

- Rahab: an actual prostitute

- Ruth: a foreigner from an enemy nation (think Russia and Ukraine or Israel and Palestine)

- Bathsheba: a woman with whom a famous king committed adultery

- Mary, Jesus' mother: a pregnant unmarried teenager (not viewed at all positively in that society)

You would think that someone who was trying to make Jesus sound like a worthy, respectable, upstanding man in a culture that cared greatly about sexual morality would try and sweep these people under the rug, rather than put them front and centre.

And Matthew had a good-sized rug that he could have swept them under, because there were plenty of heroes and kings in Jesus' line. Abraham, Jacob, Boaz, David... these names may not matter much to us today, but this is like William Shakespeare, Admiral Nelson, Martin Luther King and Nelson Mandela being in your family tree. Why doesn't Matthew just tell us about them? What made him include these women and their complicated stories?

It's almost like someone is coming to Matthew and saying, *You want me to take Jesus seriously and listen hard to his claims about who he is and what he's all about. But I've heard that he was illegitimate, and as you know in our culture that rules him out, to be honest. Can you help me with this?* And Matthew answers, *Well, I can confirm that he was born to an unmarried woman. And actually, his family line is full of scandalous situations. There's prostitution and adultery and murder too.*

Why? Partly to make this very point: Jesus was born into a messy family, in a messy world. Remember, the Bible is always very honest that there is darkness in this world. Matthew chooses to set out Jesus' family tree in the way he does to tell us three truths about this man who is at the heart of the Christian faith.

The Same but Also Very Different

The first truth is that Jesus was a real human. No family tree is truly without its difficulties and darker moments. To be really human is to be surrounded by messy realities. The only place where people get to live without complexity and difficulty is in fictional fairy stories. Matthew wants to remind us that when we read his account of Jesus' life, we're reading about a real person, born into this real world.

All humans are born. So was Jesus. All humans have a mother. So did Jesus. All humans have some dodgy relatives who you probably wouldn't talk about if you were wanting to sound impressive. So did Jesus. In this sense, he's just the same as you and me. This, Matthew is saying, is a very human story. We're dealing with the world as we experience it, not a fairy-story world where everything is simple and nice and easy.

The second truth is that there was something different about Jesus. Another odd thing that Matthew does in this family tree is to include someone who isn't an ancestor of the person at the end of the line at all. When he mentions Tamar, who lived around 18 centuries before Jesus, Matthew reminds his readers that this part-time prostitute slept with Judah, her father-in-law—and out of that most unromantic of episodes came Perez, Jesus' ancestor, and Zerah, his twin brother:

Jacob [was] the father of Judah and his brothers,
Judah the father of Perez and Zerah, whose mother
was Tamar,
Perez the father of Hezron...
                    (Matthew chapter 1, verses 2 to 3)

and so on down the generations till...

Joseph [was] the husband of Mary, and Mary was
the mother of Jesus. (v 16)

Zerah has nothing to do with the line that ran down the generations to Jesus. Why does Matthew waste ink on mentioning him?

It's because of what Zerah's and Perez's names mean. Today, most of us pick a name for our children that we like the sound of, or we name them after someone else in our family or our favourite celebrity. The name itself doesn't mean anything—it's just a combination of syllables that we like. Back then, however, names were given—and sometimes changed later on in life—to reflect the character or achievement of a person, or to encapsulate parental hopes for a person.

When these twins were born, one of them stuck his hand out first and was called Zerah, which means "rising". But then somehow the other boy barged past him and came out first, earning him the name Perez, or "breakthrough". In those two names lies a key hint about how Jesus, as well as being the same as all of us, is also different to all of us—unique, in fact.

Rising Man and Breakthrough Boy

We spend our lives trying to rise. We talk about rising up the career ladder and climbing the housing ladder. People "get to the top" in politics or sport. People will "trade up" when it comes to their car or (less excusably) their partner. All of us tend to work out where we want to get to in life, and then we work hard to raise ourselves up to that place.

Naturally speaking, then, we are all Rising Man. And if God is out there, we naturally look at our relationship with him in this way too. We see our path to God like a ladder up which we'll climb by doing enough good things. Most religions see it like that too—we're down here, God's up there, and to get to him you'll need to follow the right path, you'll need to keep the right rules, or you'll need to perform the right religious practices. We make our way up to him.

But Jesus wasn't descended from Zerah, the Rising Man. His ancestor is Perez, the Breakthrough Boy. And that ancestor's name is a nod to the remarkable claim of Christmas: that in Jesus, God broke through, into this world. God himself came from heaven, into this world. Jesus did not claim to be a man who had worked out how to get to God. He claimed to be God, who had come down to mankind, as a man. And he spent his life doing things that only God could do—controlling the weather, reversing death, manipulating time and space—to back up his claim.

This matters because there are some things that we humans just can't do on our own. Supremely, we can't find lasting peace and fulfilment—it always remains just out of reach, no matter how high we rise. We can't find a way to "rise" above our own failings and regrets, and supremely over death, and come out the other side.

But Christianity is not about us "rising" by climbing up. It is about God's "breakthrough" by climbing down—from the throne room of heaven to a feeding trough on earth. Christianity won't make any sense till we get our heads around the claim that the baby born in miraculous fashion—born not just to an unmarried woman but to an unmarried woman who had never had sex—was both completely human, just like us, and completely God, unlike us.

That's what Matthew is hinting at when he tells us that Jesus is descended from Perez, not Zerah. That's what Matthew is saying more explicitly when he says of the events leading up to Jesus' birth:

> *All this took place to fulfil what the Lord had said through the prophet: "The virgin will conceive and give birth to a son, and they will call him Immanuel" (which means "God with us"). (Matthew 1 v 22-23)*

That extraordinary idea—that when we look at Jesus, we are looking at God himself, coming to meet us in person so that we can know him—is what Matthew will show us throughout his Gospel. He wants us to see that Jesus did thoroughly human things, like sleeping and getting hungry and crying at funerals and partying at weddings, alongside thoroughly divine things, like calming storms and healing blindness and knowing the future. Jesus is not a mere human who has "risen" to the heights of wisdom, power or success; he is God, who has "broken through" to the depths of humanity.

Jesus Gets It

So Jesus is a human, just like us; he is God, not at all like us. And when we put the two together we realise a third truth: Jesus gets us, and he gives hope to us. The claim of Christmas, remember, is that Jesus is the Light, who has come from God into the darkness and difficulties of this world. This family tree is Matthew's way of saying that the Light is not just from God, but it is God himself—and that this God came to be with people like us. Not just with people who come from uncomplicated families, who have lived good lives and have nothing to be ashamed of. No, he's willing and wanting to come and live with people who are complicated, who have not always done the good thing, who know what regret feels like. He's coming to be with people like me, and like you.

Some of us have done things in the past which still haunt us years later. Some of us carry secrets we don't want anyone else to know. Some of us bear the scars of being left to bring kids up on our own, or have spent our lives trying to escape from the legacy of what happened to our family or what was done to us by our families. And Jesus says, *I'm with you. I've got a lot of that in my family.*

Not only that, but the fact that these people were part of the way that Jesus ended up being born into this world tells us that God not only understands what that's like but that he can actually work to bring good out of those situations. Jesus coming into this kind of family says that God can show mercy to and create a future for people like that. And if he can do that for them, he can do it for you. Jesus is not ashamed of failures or frightened of complexities. He even puts them in his family tree.

Jesus is unique: fully human, fully God. And he broke through from heaven to earth so that he can shine light into the messiest, most complex, most difficult places. However high you've risen or however low you feel, he broke through for you.

3

Enjoying
Christmas TV

Do you watch a TV show or movie every year as part of your Christmas tradition? Some people don't feel as if the festivities can begin until they've seen *It's a Wonderful Life*, or *The Holiday*, or *The Muppets' Christmas Carol*. I have friends who repeatedly urge me to watch *Elf*. Personally, I am much happier with *Die Hard*.

In the UK and around the Commonwealth, there is an additional televised dimension to the season—the King's Speech, broadcast at 3pm UK time on Christmas Day. The national anthem is followed by a speech from the monarch, interspersed with clips of what he has been doing that year. Everybody makes tea, sits down to watch the king for a few minutes, and then gets on with their afternoon.

When I was 17, I discovered that there are actually two King's Speeches every year, not one. There is the

Christmas broadcast, watched by millions. And then there is a formal speech read out at the annual State Opening of Parliament, watched by virtually no one. Whereas the Christmas broadcast started in 1932 (on the radio), the tradition of the monarch delivering a speech to open Parliament goes back to the 16th century and involves door-slamming, wand-waving, people walking backwards, and a Member of Parliament being held ceremonially hostage.

I only discovered the difference when I was studying history at school and heard about "the King's speech" happening in the nineteenth century. Obviously that couldn't be the Christmas Day one, I figured; so what was the teacher talking about? Fortunately Ben Thursfield said what we were all thinking: "Mr Morris, this King's Speech. Are we talking about... the Christmas one?" It was clear from Mr Morris's face that we were not. So we all laughed, secretly relieved that we had not asked the question ourselves.

And that's why, having not seen him in decades, I will think of Ben Thursfield as I settle down in front of the TV at 3pm on Christmas Day.

The Greatest Monarch

When Queen Elizabeth II died in 2022, having given 69 Christmas speeches, there was much discussion about where she ranked in terms of Britain's greatest ever ruler. In one sense, it is a ridiculous conversation; you cannot meaningfully compare an 11th-century warrior with a 21st-century constitutional monarch. But still, if I asked you, "Who is your nation's greatest ever ruler?" you would probably have an opinion about it. You might also have an opinion about the greatest ruler who has ever lived, anywhere in the world.

Today, there are a large number of candidates for that award.

But if you had asked that question in AD 1, of anyone between Spain and Syria and between the River Seine and the River Nile, there was only one right answer: Caesar Augustus.

Augustus was the ruler of the Roman Empire. Not just that; he was the greatest ruler of that empire. Born Octavian but then adopted as the son and heir of Julius Caesar, he was just 19 when his adoptive father was assassinated. In quick succession, he managed to escape being killed himself, hunt down and kill Caesar's assassins, work his way into power alongside two other men, fall out with them, beat them in battle, become supreme ruler of the entire empire, make the tax system much simpler, make the Mediterranean Sea much safer by getting rid of pirates, bring peace and prosperity to the empire after decades of civil war (the "Pax Romana"), and build a lot of straight roads.

The members of the Roman Senate were so in awe of him that, even though it was their power that he had taken, they offered him the name Augustus: the exalted one. They named a month after him, and a month after his adoptive father. (If you've ever wondered why September is the ninth month when "sept-" means seven, you can blame Julius and Augustus.) He had coins made with his face on them accompanied by the words "Augustus, son of the divine".

Consider the breathless way that people talked about him, just a few years before the first Christmas. Here's one example, from a letter written by a Roman governor:

> "It is hard to tell whether the birthday of our most divine Caesar Augustus spells more of joy or benefit, this being a date that we could probably, without fear of contradiction, equate with the beginning of all things ... he restored stability, when everything was collapsing and falling into disarray, and gave a new look to the entire world that would have been most happy to accept its own ruin had not the good and common fortune of all been born: Caesar Augustus ... Providence has filled Augustus with divine power for the benefit of humanity, and in her beneficence has granted us and those who will come after us a Saviour who has made war to cease and who shall put everything in peaceful order ... The birthday of our god signalled the beginning of good news for the world because of him."

So, who is the greatest ruler of all time? Caesar Augustus. Why? Because he is the Saviour of the world.

Because he restored stability when everything was collapsing. Because he gave a new look to the entire world. Because he has brought wars to an end and made peace everywhere. His birth "signalled the beginning of good news for the world".

He is nothing less than the answer to the world's problems. He is the Saviour.

An Emperor and a Baby

So we are somewhere around AD 1 (although nobody called it that then, of course), and pretty much the entire known world is ruled by a man who has shown himself to be strong, who has brought peace, who has helped you towards prosperity. All he asks is your loyalty and obedience, and he will give you everything you need.

And he decides to count everyone in his empire. Which he can do, because he has the power to move people with a simple command:

In those days Caesar Augustus issued a decree that a census should be taken of the entire Roman world. (This was the first census that took place while Quirinius was governor of Syria.) And everyone went to their own town to register. (Luke 2 v 1-3)

This is how Luke—an early Christian historian who wrote a two-volume narrative based on written sources and eyewitness interviews—tells it. That's the power that this single man had. And then Luke moves his focus from the most powerful person in the world to one of the weakest:

So Joseph also went up from the town of Nazareth in Galilee to Judea, to Bethlehem the town of David, because he belonged to the house and line of David. He went there to register with Mary, who was pledged to be married to him and was expecting a child. While they were there, the time came for the baby to be born, and she gave birth to her firstborn, a son. She wrapped him in cloths and placed him in a manger, because there was no guest room available for them. (v 3-7)

A baby. Homeless. No name as yet. A Jew on the margins of the empire, in Bethlehem, the "house of bread". Born out of wedlock to a random couple. If you were to read this to someone in the first century and ask them, "Who in this story is the greatest ruler, the saviour?" there is only one sensible answer. And it's not the baby in the feeding trough.

Everyone would agree on that. Except the angels.

Good News of Great Joy
Here's how the angels—God's messengers—saw things that night:

And an angel of the Lord appeared to [some nearby shepherds], and the glory of the Lord shone around them, and they were filled with fear. And the angel said to them, "Fear not, for behold, I bring you good news of great joy that will be for all the people. For unto you is born this day in the city of David a Saviour, who is Christ the Lord. And this will be a sign for you: you will find a baby wrapped in swaddling cloths and lying in a manger." And suddenly there was with the angel a multitude of the heavenly host praising God and saying,

*"Glory to God in the highest,
    and on earth peace among those with whom he is pleased!" (v 9-14, ESV)*

The angels use all the great slogans of the day. Here is a birth that brings "good news of great joy". Here is a Saviour. Here is peace in human form. But they're not talking about Augustus. They're talking about Jesus.

So here's something to consider: how can the angels possibly have been right? After all, when he grew up this baby never held power. He never led an army. He never wrote a book or made coins bearing his inscription. He never left his homeland, a backwater on the edge of the empire. At the peak of his popularity, his followers numbered in the low thousands, and that number quickly dwindled again to just over a hundred by the time he died. He finished his life as a condemned criminal, executed for opposing the mighty Augustus, with hardly a friend in the world.

Luke is deliberately putting these two men side by side and asking us: Which of these two candidates for kingship, for divinity, for being the saviour of the world, for being viewed as the person who fixes what is most broken and provides what we most need, looks like the real deal? Which one can truly save? Who are you going to back?

August Promises

The world is still full of Augustus-type rulers. Even if emperors have fallen out of fashion for now, we still want leaders who will address the problems we face. We still look for Augustus-type saviours. We want someone in charge who will bring victory and provide stability. We want someone who will bring peace. We want someone who will bring prosperity. We want this "new look"—for the flaws and failings of the previous regime to be banished and replaced with something better, bigger, more full of hope. That's what the world wants. That's how our politicians position themselves: "Look at what is wrong. Then look to me because I can fix it; I can save you from it."

So the eighteenth-century French revolutionaries promised, "Liberté, Egalité, Fraternité" (Freedom, Equality, Brotherhood). The early-twentieth-century Russian revolutionaries offered, "Peace, Land and Bread". After the First World War, British politicians went for "A Land Fit for Heroes". And promises like that continue into the present. "Yes We Can." "Take Back Control." "Get Brexit Done." "Make America Great Again."

Even as we look for this kind of leader, we know deep down that however excited we get, no leader ever really delivers on their promises. Ours is a fairly weary, cynical age, partly because political leaders have so often not lived up to their own hype. Even Augustus, despite all the propaganda, failed to deliver on his. But there is a bigger problem than over-promising and under-delivering. It is that the promises themselves are not ambitious enough.

Think about them for a moment. You can have peace; you can get rid of pirates; you can have a simpler tax system; you can have straight roads; you can have prosperity. You can leave the European Union or construct a big wall between the US and Mexico. Some of these offers will sound more compelling to you than others—but no matter how ambitious they are, they do not get to the heart of what is wrong with the world. Our problems run deeper than pirates, taxes or the EU. We need saving from darkness, from death—and no leader we can find can deliver that.

Enter the other Saviour. The one in the manger.

Christmas Presence

"Jesus"—or "Yeshua" in Hebrew, the ancient language of his people—sounds very ordinary when compared with "Augustus". Among first-century Jews it was a common name for a boy; it meant "Yahweh saves". Today it is familiar to most English-speaking people as a swear word. But in Matthew's Gospel we hear the explosive, world-changing promise behind that choice of name. "You are to give him the name Jesus," the angel tells Mary's fiancé, Joseph, "because he will save his people from their sins" (Matthew 1 v 21).

It is an astonishing claim. This child can save you from all of your sins: all of the evils you have committed against God and against other people, and all of the good things you should have done and failed to. He has come to scrub clean all of your stains, pay off all your debts, compensate for all your flaws. God has become like you, and he is going to live the life you should have lived—a life of moral perfection, compassion, joy and love—and then, at the cross, die the death you should have died, before rising from the tomb and overcoming the power of death. This changes everything. Your sins can be forgiven. Your darkness can turn to light. Death itself can start working backwards.

God knows our needs better than we do. If our biggest problem was taxes, roads or pirates, then God would have sent us an "Augustus": a bureaucrat or an engineer, a general or a politician. But it isn't. Our biggest problem is that our sin has separated us from God, that "the wages of sin is death" (Romans 6 v 23), and so we face a spiritual death beyond our physical death—an existence with nothing good and nothing to look forward to. So God has sent us a "Jesus", who will save his people from their sins and save them into a life of joy, love, peace, and hope with him.

Rescue from sin and death is such a central aspect of Jesus' work that it appears everywhere in the Gospels. But here is the clearest way to see it—read the stories of Jesus' death on the cross. Listen to this King's speech.

Jesus suffers the curse that our sins deserve: "My God, my God, why have you forsaken me?" (Mark 15 v 34).

We receive the forgiveness that we don't deserve: "Father, forgive them, for they do not know what they are doing" (Luke 23 v 34).

Our debt is settled by the only one with enough credit to clear it: "It is finished" (John 19 v 30).

He is forsaken. We can be forgiven. It is finished.

Which Rescuer?

So who is the true rescuer: Augustus the "Exalted" or Jesus the "Saviour"? Augustus fought his political and military rivals and won; but Jesus fought sin and death and won. Augustus drove out pirates and reformed the taxes; but Jesus drove out sickness and reformed the human heart.

Who is the greatest? There is a clue in our calendar. Yes, the month of August is named after the Roman emperor who ruled when Luke wrote his book. But the years are numbered after the birth-date of the baby

Luke wrote his book about. On New Year's Day, when you first write down the number of the new year (and have to concentrate on getting it right), that will be a reminder that the boy from the house of bread changed history far more profoundly than the emperor in the capital city.

It could also be a reminder that Jesus was born to save you from your biggest problem, and for the life you long for.

4

Making Memories

Part of the fun of this time of year is looking back on previous Christmases and recalling all the memorable incidents of past Decembers—especially the ones which didn't go according to plan. The time I forgot to put the brake on my baby son's buggy (stroller), and he rolled into the lake. (He was fine.) The Christmas it was so windy that we literally couldn't open the car door to get out. The year I made fun of my father-in-law's cooking and was made to eat dinner in the garden on my own.

While writing this book, I went over to my next-door neighbour and asked for his favourite Christmas memory. Without hesitating, he told me about the year that a man in a rugby shirt had gone to church with his family on Christmas Day covered in blood, because his girlfriend had just hit him over the head with a hammer.

I have had my Christmas gatecrashed by an unexpected guest too. Admittedly it did not involve a hammer—but it did involve a hamster. Our neighbours (the same ones, as it happens) were away over Christmas and had asked us to look after their pets. Dutifully we popped over each day to check on the hamster and the chickens. But on Christmas Day, we realised that something very odd had happened to the hamster. It was—and there is no other word for this— flat. I don't mean that it was smaller than usual. I mean that it looked like it had been ironed. It could have been a collapsed souffle.

We never found out how it died. It doesn't really matter. But that's how I ended up performing a surreal burial ceremony on Christmas Day in my neighbours' garden, trying to make sure I wasn't spotted by any children who might possibly have been traumatised by the sight. The unexpected guest who hijacked my Christmas and provided me with another favourite Christmas memory was a dead hamster.

Unexpected guests (living, non-bloodied, non-flat ones) lie at the heart of the first Christmas too.

How the Story Doesn't Go

Imagine for a moment that the Christian story is true. Imagine that the God who inspired the Old Testament and who had been making and keeping promises to the Jews for centuries, finally sent his Son to be their king:

their Light, their Immanuel, their Saviour. The King is born, the angels announce it, some shepherds who happen to be (a) awake and (b) nearby go and see him, and then…

Who, would you predict, would be the next people to find him and pay their respects to him?

Surely it would be a group of observant, zealous and religious Jews who know the Scriptures and long for the Christ, the divinely-promised King?

That's how the story should go. But that's exactly how it doesn't unfold. Have a look at what Matthew tells us about who comes to see Jesus and what they do when they find him—and who doesn't go to see Jesus, even after they find out about him:

> *After Jesus was born in Bethlehem in Judea, during the time of King Herod, Magi from the east came to Jerusalem and asked, "Where is the one who has been born king of the Jews? We saw his star when it rose and have come to worship him."*

> *When King Herod heard this he was disturbed, and all Jerusalem with him. When he had called together all the people's chief priests and teachers of the law, he asked them where the Messiah was to be born. "In Bethlehem in Judea," they replied, "for this is what the prophet has written:*

> *"'But you, Bethlehem, in the land of Judah,*
> *are by no means least among the rulers of Judah;*

for out of you will come a ruler
who will shepherd my people Israel.'"

Then Herod called the Magi secretly and found out
from them the exact time the star had appeared. He
sent them to Bethlehem and said, "Go and search
carefully for the child. As soon as you find him,
report to me, so that I too may go and worship him."

After they had heard the king, they went on their
way, and the star they had seen when it rose went
ahead of them until it stopped over the place where
the child was. When they saw the star, they were
overjoyed. On coming to the house, they saw the
child with his mother Mary, and they bowed down
and worshipped him. Then they opened their
treasures and presented him with gifts of gold,
frankincense and myrrh. And having been warned
in a dream not to go back to Herod, they returned to
their country by another route. (Matthew 2 v 1-12)

Here is Matthew, a Jew, writing an account for Jewish
readers of a man who he says is the King of the Jews.
And it is non-Jews who worship him first.

The Unexpected Guests

There's a famous carol that confidently tells us that the
men at the centre of this part of the story were "three
kings" who came from the "orient". Tradition tells
us what their names were and that they came riding

camels. But Matthew tells us none of that—he tells us very little at all about them.

We don't know their names.

We don't know how they arrived.

We don't know how many of them there were.

We just know that these are precisely not the people we would expect to worship "the King of the Jews". They are from another country, somewhere in the distant "east". They are from another culture. They are almost certainly from another religion. (There's no indication that they knew the Old Testament—if they did, they'd already have known that God had promised that this coming king was going to be born in Bethlehem, rather than in Jerusalem.) Here are the most unexpected guests possible.

And yet here they come, travelling a long way, turning up unannounced and refusing to head home till they have found "the one who has been born king of the Jews". Here they are, when they find him, kneeling and giving him the best gifts they can offer.

Meanwhile, the Jewish religious leaders, who know their Bibles really well, are... staying in Jerusalem. Instead of going to find out whether God's promised King has been born in Bethlehem, they stay in the capital, pandering to King Herod, who (plot spoiler) is working out how to have Jesus killed.

It's the equivalent of Jesus being born today and Christian theologians and pastors—people like me—

being so preoccupied with our power and privilege and influence that we don't even notice he's come, while the first people who find him and worship him are Islamic fundamentalists who saw him in a dream or tribal witch-doctors who have worked out he's come by studying the bones of their ancestors. Because we're used to seeing the wise men on the front of our Christmas cards, we completely miss how unexpected and weird it is that they were there at all.

The King for Everyone

You may think, "So what?" (Unless you're an Islamic fundamentalist or a witch-doctor.) Well, the point is that Jesus is King for everyone. Jesus came for everyone. He's not just King for the Jews; he's King for people who come from somewhere in Asia to worship him. He's king for people who come from Africa—from the continent he spent his earliest years living in. He's King for people who come from lands beyond the world Matthew knew about—from the strange, misty island of Britain or from the undiscovered (by Eurasians) continents of America and Australia. He's King for good modern democrats who may not think they even need one, but who still recognise deep down that their deepest needs cannot be met by wealth or education or influence and that they might need something (or someone) more.

This means that if you're someone who has always thought of yourself as being a long way away from

Jesus and Christianity, the wise men showing up is a wonderful invitation for you. Perhaps you're from a culture that has little room for Christian things. Perhaps you were born in a country where Jesus is of little consequence. Perhaps you have lived a life that didn't have any room for Jesus.

None of that needs to stop you coming. If you're starting to realise that this Jesus might just be the Light that you need, the God you need, the Saviour you need, then nothing in your background means you're uninvited. Often the people who most clearly see how exciting the coming of Jesus is are those who have only just encountered him.

In fact, Matthew's account is most challenging not to those who didn't grow up as "religious Christians" but to those who did. If you are someone who has always gone to church, who has tended to be surrounded by echoes of Jesus in your culture, and who tends to live according to the rules laid out in the Bible, then pause for a moment. The religious leaders in Jesus' day were just like that. And they missed him. So it might be worth checking that you're not staying in Jerusalem, so to speak. It is possible to be unwilling to give up the positions and comforts you've built up in your life, and therefore to hold back from coming to Jesus and worshipping him as your King.

But whoever we are and wherever we're from, our response to Jesus doesn't change who he is (any more than Herod's rejection of him or the wise men's acceptance of him did). Jesus' reign is not subject to a vote. It wouldn't threaten his position even if the whole world turned into Herods, denying and defying his rule. "The light shines in the darkness," remember, "and the darkness has not overcome it" (John 1 v 5).

That's a good thing because, as we've seen, he's the ruler we need: the ruler who can do for us what no one else can. But it's also a challenging truth because no matter how many people believe him or follow him, Jesus is the King. He is the King of the Jews. He is the King of the non-Jews. He is the King.

The King over Everything

In fact, Jesus is King over the whole universe. That comes clearly through the Christmas story. Earthly rulers like Herod and Caesar are subject to the King of kings, in all their plotting and census-taking (all of which is used by God to achieve his wider purposes). So are wise men from the east, bowing down and worshipping the King of the Jews. So are angels, who appear on the scene with a regularity that makes it seem normal. So are the stars, whose position and movement in the sky guide the wise men. So are the subconscious minds of men and women, whose dreams shape the story in profound ways. To this day, the "kings" of the world rise and fall—Henry VIII, Queen Victoria, Josef Stalin, Idi Amin, Donald

Trump—but the child "who has been born king of the Jews" reigns for ever.

This truth also comes through clearly in the Easter story. In many ways, that is where the lordship of this King of kings is made most visible. Jesus' story starts with a miracle—life in a virgin's womb. And it finishes with a miracle—life in a corpse's tomb. As Jesus, having been dead for three days, keeps the promise he'd made multiple times to his friends and steps out of his own grave and appears to hundreds of people over the next few weeks, he is hailed not just as "Saviour" but as "Lord": as Master, Sovereign, King, Final Authority. "My Lord and my God!" cries his friend Thomas, who had refused to believe Jesus was alive after his death until Jesus came and stood right in front of him, which put an end to the argument (John 20 v 27-28). "All authority in heaven and on earth has been given to me," declares Jesus in the final "King's Speech" in Matthew's Gospel. Sure, Herod might rule Judea, but he is no match for death. Augustus might have conquered everywhere from Spain to Syria, but he could never conquer the grave. Jesus did. He's King even over death.

All That Matters Is the King

A couple of years ago, I taught my son Sam how to play chess. I explained how all the different pieces move and what each of the different pieces are worth. He would get very excited whenever he took one of my pieces and very worried when it looked like I would take one of his.

The thing I kept explaining to him, but which he found hard to grasp, was this: in chess, ultimately, all that matters is the king. As long as your king stands, no matter how many pieces you have lost, the game continues. If you lose your king, no matter how many pieces you have won, then you lose. All that matters is the king.

That is the great declaration of Christmas. There is a King: a King who reigns over this world, over this universe, over all that is unseen, for ever. There is a King who offers to save you from sin and death, so that you can enjoy peace under his perfect rule, for ever.

If this is true, then as long as you have him as your king, life continues and victory is assured. Equally, if you don't, then it doesn't really matter how the other pieces of your life are going. We can get very distracted with or motivated by the ups and downs of this move or that little victory. But, at the end of the day, all that matters is the King.

So the question that Christmas poses for all of us—whatever our culture, our religion, our upbringing—is: is Jesus my King? Are the priorities of your life determined ultimately by you or by him? Are your decisions—moral, ethical, relational, sexual, financial—directed by you or by him? If you are willing to lay down your self-rule and your efforts to rise up—your attempts to get what you need in life in your own strength—then there will be times when you feel like you are winning and succeeding, and there'll be times when you feel like you are losing, and there'll be times when you're not sure which is happening. But in the end, you will know that you have the Light, that God is with you, and that you are saved. Why? Because the King still stands, and that's all that matters.

At that first Christmas, some very surprising people from a very surprising background decided to come and worship Jesus as their King.

This Christmas, you could make the same decision.

What Next?

Thank you so much for reading this. I hope it has helped you think through the meaning of your Christmas, the meaning of the first Christmas, and how they are connected.

But you may be asking the question: what next? For a number of people in the Christmas story, the answer was obvious: go to Bethlehem, find Jesus, and discover whether the news they had been told was true. For people today, that isn't the answer! So if we want to find out more, what do we do now?

The first thing I would suggest you do is to read one of the Gospels in the New Testament. There are four—Matthew, Mark, Luke and John—and you can easily find them in shops or online. Mark is the shortest, and probably the easiest one to read if you are new to Christianity. John is the deepest and most mysterious, which makes him lots of people's favourite. Luke is the longest and the most historically detailed. Matthew is my personal favourite, but then I'm odd like that. Whichever one you choose, read it all; it will take you between two and four hours in total. Trust me: you won't want to miss the ending.

The second thing to do is to visit a church that takes the Bible seriously as the word of God. You could pitch up on a Sunday, which new people do at my church every week. Or you could go on a short course designed to help people investigate whether Christianity is true, like the Alpha Course, Christianity Explored, or 3-2-1. Most good churches will run something like this, and you'll meet others who have similar questions to yours.

And the third thing is to pray. Ask God to speak to you as you read the Gospels, to help you understand his purpose for your life and to reveal himself to you. Thank him for the good things he has given you and ask him to help you with the challenges you're facing. If you haven't prayed before, a great place to start is the prayer that Jesus taught his disciples:

Our Father in heaven,
Hallowed be your name,
May your kingdom come,
May your will be done:
On earth, as in heaven!
Give us today our daily bread,
And forgive us our sins,
As we forgive those who sin against us.
And lead us not into temptation,
But deliver us from evil.
Amen.

Merry Christmas!

thegoodbook
COMPANY

Thanks for reading this book. We hope you enjoyed it, and found it helpful.

Most people want to find answers to the big questions of life: Who are we? Why are we here? How should we live? But for many valid reasons we are often unable to find the time or the right space to think positively and carefully about them.

Perhaps you have questions that you need an answer for. Perhaps you have met Christians who have seemed unsympathetic or incomprehensible. Or maybe you are someone who has grown up believing, but need help to make things a little clearer.

At The Good Book Company, we're passionate about producing materials that help people of all ages and stages understand the heart of the Christian message, which is found in the pages of the Bible.

Whoever you are, and wherever you are at when it comes to these big questions, we hope we can help. As a publisher we want to help you look at the good book that is the Bible because we're convinced that as we meet the person who stands at its heart—Jesus Christ—we find the clearest answers to our biggest questions.

Visit our website to discover the range of books, videos and other resources we produce, or visit our partner site www.christianityexplored.org for a clear explanation of who Jesus is and why he came.

Thanks again for reading,

Your friends at The Good Book Company

thegoodbook.com | thegoodbook.co.uk
thegoodbook.com.au | thegoodbook.co.nz | thegoodbook.co.in

WWW.CHRISTIANITYEXPLORED.ORG

Our partner site is a great place to explore the Christian faith, with powerful testimonies and answers to difficult questions.